Flying through a Hole in the Storm

Hollis Summers Poetry Prize

GENERAL EDITOR: JILL ROSSER

Named after the distinguished poet who taught for many years at Ohio University and made Athens, Ohio, the subject of many of his poems, this competition invites writers to submit unpublished collections of original poems. The competition is open to poets who have not published a book-length collection as well as to those who have.

Full and updated information is available on the Hollis Summers Poetry Prize web page: ohioswallow.com/poetry_prize.

Meredith Carson, *Infinite Morning*
Memye Curtis Tucker, *The Watchers*
V. Penelope Pelizzon, *Nostos*
Kwame Dawes, *Midland*
Allison Eir Jenks, *The Palace of Bones*
Robert B. Shaw, *Solving for X*
Dan Lechay, *The Quarry*
Joshua Mehigan, *The Optimist*
Jennifer Rose, *Hometown for an Hour*
Ann Hudson, *The Armillary Sphere*
Roger Sedarat, *Dear Regime: Letters to the Islamic Republic*
Jason Gray, *Photographing Eden*
Will Wells, *Unsettled Accounts*
Stephen Kampa, *Cracks in the Invisible*
Nick Norwood, *Gravel and Hawk*
Charles Hood, *South x South: Poems from Antarctica*
Alison Powell, *On the Desire to Levitate*
Shane Seely, *The Surface of the Lit World*
Michelle Y. Burke, *Animal Purpose*
Michael Shewmaker, *Penumbra*
Idris Anderson, *Doubtful Harbor*
Joseph J. Capista, *Intrusive Beauty*
Julie Hanson, *The Audible and the Evident*
Fleda Brown, *Flying through a Hole in the Storm*

Flying through a Hole in the Storm

Poems

Fleda Brown

OHIO UNIVERSITY PRESS

ATHENS

Ohio University Press, Athens, Ohio 45701
ohioswallow.com
© 2021 by Fleda Brown
All rights reserved

Printed in the United States of America
Ohio University Press books are printed on acid-free paper ∞ ™

31 30 29 28 27 26 25 24 23 22 21 5 4 3 2 1

Library of Congress Cataloging-in-Publication Data
Names: Jackson, Fleda Brown, 1944– author.
Title: Flying through a hole in the storm : poems / Fleda Brown.
Description: Athens : Ohio University Press, [2021] | Series: Hollis summers
poetry prize
Identifiers: LCCN 2020045775 (print) | LCCN 2020045776 (ebook) | ISBN
9780821424445 (paperback) | ISBN 9780821447369 (pdf)
Subjects: LCGFT: Poetry.
Classification: LCC PS3560.A21534 F59 2021 (print) | LCC PS3560.A21534
(ebook) | DDC 811/.54–dc23
LC record available at https://lccn.loc.gov/2020045775
LC ebook record available at https://lccn.loc.gov/2020045776

For Jerry

Contents

I

Not Dying

False prophecy of this
hour, when I come closer, you ease
away. . . .

—Yusef Komunyakaa

Come Moths

Come moths
to the sticky triangular tents I have placed
in the closet, in the pantry, come down
with your tiny paper wings and brown
anonymity. Come uncatchable loose flecks
of the universe, come smudges,
come floaters in the eye,
mispunctuated sentences, misappropriated funds.
Gather into the dark. Let me be free of holes
in the weave, let me be free even
of the idea of mistake. Come moths
to your natural doom and I to mine, for you
have already eaten through
what I had chosen to wear, what I had hoped.
You have made me see the light.
Now we are together in this, finishing
each other, pro and con.

Wakened by Crows

In the woods, the sky
        of our sleep breaking,
piece by piece. Nothing visible
        in the leaves but the blackness
moving gradually off as light
        starts to ping back its notice.

My father would caw
        and the crows would answer,
and he'd stand there like a boy,
        shit-grin-delighted,
caw-caw, caw-caw.
        This is left, this is left,
of the old life, is what he heard.
        You could see it
in his eyes. He shot a crow
        once, for no reason, he said,
and he cried at its dense black,
        its perfectly curved beak.

I was a child, listening,
        waiting to be seen,
but it was only the calling,
        and the voice was air,
and the air was nothing
        human, and I was standing
under the pines and hemlocks.
        How hard it was,
this is what I want to say, to wake
        from that disappearing,
to answer the old life
        with this one.

It Isn't That You Forget Things

If you were gauging where they are, you could use the map Enbridge puts out
to show how far under Lake Michigan the oil pipeline would go.
Deep enough to be safe,
                    is the idea,

although you know nothing is safe, and what you hold now will corrode
and eventually break through.

There is nothing under your bones. Think about that.
If you go deep, it is all marrow and bone, and then you come out the other side.

When she was in a hurry, my mother would call all her children's names.
Names also run together as the membrane gets thinner.

When a name finally appears, it is like a trophy. Too late, you come up with
a mnemonic device. You try to remember a way to remember the device.

When you say the word over and over, it is gradually absorbed like yeast into dough.
It is not possible to retrieve it. It has become who you are

which is quite complex, if anyone wanted to investigate.
For example, Lake Michigan-Huron is the same lake,

shallow and narrow at the Straits, and freezes in the winter.
Ice might remember when it was soft and moved in its multiple ways,

when it could be this lake or that, but that cannot be tested
in present conditions.

The things I remember are below the level of sorting out.
                    They are so deep they are like love. Inarticulate,
thrashing around when they need to speak.

Museum

Streaming-hair woman wanders the hallway
     in flowered nightgown, *Where is my family?*
Where is my mother? When will they come? Led back

to her room again and again. When the body dies slowly,
     the mind lives a museum version.
When Eisenhower was president everyone had a mother,

Mamie wore her serviceable pearl necklace and
     nobody needed to be gorgeous because
there was work to do and the pill hadn't been invented

so action and consequence were one,
     and the sidewalk was cracked. Trees
and houses were huger than they would ever

be again, tadpoles squiggled, and the rest took care
     of itself. I don't know when it was
that the mighty structures began to live inside me

and I myself became the nation and the wind
     began howling and the gut of the nation
began rumbling. I will tell you a story:

Once upon a time there were world wars,
     the Korean War, there was McCarthy,
there was terror and confusion, there was Al Capone,

even, and it seemed that would never end.
     How would it end? It ended
in newspaper words, gathered like a squirrel's nest

in winter, a blob on a branch so high
                    it seemed impossible. Even
in Eisenhower's time: squirrels. And you wonder

how long the experiment of your life will continue
                    while water quivers and wood
rots and the museum is erected, everything's

explained on a plaque. "Don't be scared,"
                    we'd said to each other in the dark,
but nothing happened except this living.

And Eisenhower, bald, canonical, moved far
                    out of reach, and the woman
wandering the hallway, opening door after door,

is checking to see if America has finally
                    come back from its long, long trip.

Milkweed

I love the way milkweeds open their mouths
        to let themselves out, even if they sometimes
                look like they scream against their will.
I love the way tufts of themselves grab on to
        nearby stalks to keep the neighborhood strong.
            The stalks remain upright
in spite of their hollowness. Everything is hollow
        in a good way. Everything has finished its job
            and has moved on to the next thing.
It is all a tangle, as if a mighty wind
        had come through. I can only tell you about this
            from out here. Something has come undone
in me, maybe it happened centuries ago. My mind
        has run off with the evidence.
            I don't know how to talk about this.
All I can say is when I see the milkweed in its bliss
        of shedding, I want to hold you to me forever,
            which is the wrong thing. I have somehow
come undone from the shedding and have wandered off
        into the stories my mind came up with
            to explain why I should live forever.

Glasses

Quickly came the mudslide, turned the air
  the thickness of pudding in the mouth, the ears, the hands.
    The glasses slid to somewhere

and were found, picked out of the sludge,
  the worker picked them out of the sludge, came upon this
    intimacy like brushing back a hair

from a face, something that doesn't want
  intruders, came upon this artifact, like a name, only not.
    Her particular myopia, corrected.

He took them, that spoke for the actual body,
  His mind ferrying itself back and forth across
    the life-death border until it felt like

gossamer. What I imagined, reading this. Because of
  these other glasses. I feel the border, not a border
    but a sliding, there it goes,

like that, an avalanche of suddenness, being only the suddenness
  of seeing: I take my father's glasses,
    glasses edged with superglue,

string wrapped around the hinge, smeared
  with glue, his clever repair. I take them up
    and fit them for him over the hearing aids,

the oxygen tube. They will be left. Everything comes and goes.
  Something is left. Someone is left
    holding the still-concave space.

Nothing Comes Together to Mean What I Meant

The old men in the front office of Don's Auto Repair
with its oily-mechanical smell,
the old men in their pale jackets go on
with their talk, not yet seeing me, their soft crumple
and grumble the edge of a far storm.
I can't tell you how it is a loss, an admonition,
as I make my awkward entrance,
with my exactitude about tire pressure,
my language like arrows.
They are smiling benevolently
at my intrusion, wishing it to be
no longer than necessary, sending me into the guts
of the shop where Don is under a grandly
suspended truck, with all the hammering,
and the radio turned up. I am to break through
this and be heard. If I stand there,
I'm stupid. If I shout, I interrupt his concentration
on rotors or crankshaft, names that come to me
as I hope to fit in, as always. I am preparing
a speech about my decreased tire pressure, its history,
the puzzling nature of its recurrence.
I am preparing a speech.
Years go by. Whatsoever is tender and lost
in me grows ever more patient, while sparks
are flying from under the truck and the old men
behind the shut door pause now and then
to rummage in their shirt pockets for the cigarettes
they know very well they no longer smoke.

Afternoons at the Lake

I would rather be trapped in an attic with rats than play Monopoly
all the afternoons it takes to lose the last of my money to the already

superrich 1-percent grandchild, to line up cheap green houses
on my low-rent Baltic and Mediterranean Avenues in a futile attempt

to collect enough to survive the next round of rent on Boardwalk
or Park Place, to feel pitiful gratitude when I Receive for Services

twenty-five dollars. Everything will be gone, save the smallest
denominations, the Asian crayfish will overrun the native,

the autumn olive will proliferate, the tallest thing will grow taller,
will be layered with gold, will turn to gold, will harden its gold heart.

It will squander, jet, pocket, dole, win past wanting to win, dig
the mineshaft, the ore, eat up the hillside the birds the whales,

crack the foundations of houses, force the defaulters into the street.
Dice will land as they will, will cause the tiny car to bounce

happily from St. James Place to Indiana Avenue, a galaxy of gobble,
will enable the placement of flamboyant hotels on the coast

where waters wash with exquisite music shoreward, all of it owned
by the God who dwells inside the winning, who has not said

otherwise yet, who owns Free Parking and Jail, who owns the treeless
board, the classy neighborhoods as well as the ones with the rats

and smashed-out windows, the murderous scrawl of languages
on walls, the smiling God holding the center with top hat and cane,

as I at last step out on the dock with my coffee and say to myself
the lines where Keats rhymes "think" with "nothingness do sink."

Not Dying

He says he wakes and it feels momentarily
like he's finally dying, a giving way, a sinking
or hovering, can't say, but momentary: a window swung
open you don't realize until a breeze.

I take him for a ride along the tongue
of land, west looking east, looking back at the city
from a point. Jet trails. He points them out, strung
like necklaces, one fresh, with its glint out front.

We talk glaciers, how they stuttered and glinted
down Michigan, pools for each pause,
those excellent lapses. And branches bare because
the trees are all dead, he says, forgetting the time of year.

No, I say, dormant. Road hum. Ducks with their flawless wake.
It hurts to turn his head. I slow and turn. Each new thing
needs to be dead center, unencumbered. The names:
mallard, jet trail, Power Island. Boat slips claim

blank water breathing in their hollows. He says it feels
like dying, he says it as if he had been lit up from the inside,
a room waiting, a waiting room. Not an ordeal,
but road hum and light.

At night the aides come by. One kisses him goodnight
on the lips, he says. Where? The lips. He smiles
as if he's gotten away with something. He's miles
away, a faint agreeable aftertaste. Nothing he can describe.

Dear Pablo Picasso

I wadded up the newspaper, the news wadded up the paper, the paper was all black and white with screaming and breaking, it was Guernica, crying and dying and I did not know how to stop the tearing along the seams. The presses had pressed the ink teeth and jaws and horses and an eyeball light bulb was watching at the top. I thought it was God watching political systems breaking down, every man for himself, every woman for herself. I write this to ask you if light bulb God has compassion or forgiveness or is forever simply burning until even the power plant is bombed. I ask you if you made God's spiked eyelashes to lash out. The world is lashing out, the wars have lost their names. Did you think you could redeem anything by art, did you think you could put the tears in before they dried and fell like leaves? The mouths are open. They are beyond expecting help. I was staring at the shards and seeing how they fit together as if I were God seeing how the whole has a quality of doneness, light and shadow, angle and curve.

Ode on Terror

I used to think that whole yellow-line
        thing between me and oncoming
trucks was natural, before they started
        swerving across sidewalks, across
center islands. Also, I've become aware
        that the complicated organs
necessary to allow me even one more
        breath could refuse to collude
anymore. The way I see it, the cracks
        in logic are all filled with gunpowder.
When I want to see terror up close,
        I remember chemo, radiation.
There it is, the word, slathering
        everything with implications:
Tear and *Roar*. You can see the teeth,
        you can hear the barking dog.
You can't see the thoughts that caused
        the killings, the bombings,
flying loose, thumbing against the sky,
        so nothing is safe. You could hide
under the duvet where the truck roar
        would be muted. Still, those
people on the sidewalk! Sitting ducks!
        Walking around so full of love
terror is going to have to rip them wide
        open, like dissecting a frog
to see what makes it jump.

Sing

Through here, she said. Inside the chapel were narrow concrete stairs, which we climbed to the first landing. She had presented this as a secret, which I promised to keep. Stop, she said. Sing, she said. I can't, I said. Anything, she said, so I started in on "We Are Climbing Jacob's Ladder." The sound wasn't an echo but a softening and a carrying as if my voice were wind and the walls had held it for a hundred years at last releasing it slowly, like blood into water. I imagined I did not exist, that the sound was always loose, it was my imagination that I had made it myself. Climb higher, she said, so we did. I found her abrupt childlike attentions intriguing. We made a flute of the stairwell or some instrument not yet invented that opens the pores and makes singers of us. I was a child who could sing anything, the voice something like a headstone, substance standing for lack of it. One step followed another, summer came, the coats pushed back in the closet, flowers bloomed, first the buttercups, then hyacinths, tulips, and finally the fierce daylilies one after the other as if we were moving from a very low place to a higher which could easily be explained by the transit of the sun, or rather, the earth's relation to it. It was impossible to form any judgment, which I recognized as love, that I loved her better than most in some secret way. My voice came out in those colors and we sang "Tell Me Why," "Ol' Man River," the few whole songs I could remember, but she knew them all, being a singer. Still, I was not embarrassed, being a child with few moral judgments sitting on the spillway at church camp with maybe 80 percent of my life still strung out somewhere glittering, encased in some twilit dawn. Nothing else, except we agreed to bring music next time, to have more words, the way things go, toward professionalism, the way water is sent down a spillway stone by stone so as not to overwhelm the landscape.

II

Treatises

The Feet, mechanical, go round—
A Wooden way
Of Ground, or Air, or Ought—
Regardless grown,
A Quartz contentment, like a stone—

—Emily Dickinson

Treatises

On Butterflies

I have not seen a butterfly yet this spring. There are fewer and
fewer, yet I can send you a text message with many little blue
ones, in a row. King Midas in the Greek legend turned everything
he touched to solid gold, which turned out to be not so good if
you wanted a drink of water, or if you longed for a real butterfly's
airy flutter at the edge of your sight. If you longed for the spiritual
world. It is good to remember that the spiritual world was first
made out of chewed leaves, then suspended in a chrysalis like a
dream for a great long while before it knew what it had become.
That is like this grief since my father died. Who knows how long
I will hang here, or if what comes next will be any improvement.
Who said the butterfly is more spiritual than the worm, anyway?
Is it better to fly than to crawl? I have so many questions, being
stuck here, as I am. It feels as if my father is fluttering at the edge
of my sight, but that's the habit of my mind. No single butterfly
completes a long migration, sometimes it takes six generations. He
was lying there pale as a statue, which is the dying phase of living.
Some people see a butterfly and think it is their beloved dead
sending a message from beyond. When one phase is over, I think
it is natural to start looking around to see what kind of outfit life is
going to be wearing next.

On Dreams

It might be that you think you're living your life and then find
you've waked up like in *The Matrix* to a grittier one, that your actual
body is a part of, and you will have to feel everything. The average
person has four or five dreams a night. After sex dreams, anxiety
dreams are the most common. In my dreams I am often trying to
get somewhere. I am floating across the campus like a butterfly. I

have forgotten my clothes, I am going to show up late and my class will have left. I am surprised in my dream that the students glance at me only as a curiosity. I have a certain translucency. The platypus dreams up to eight hours a day. That is, it has that much rapid eye movement. Imagine what is trapped under there. Imagine the fragments like floaters. In daytime, the floaters are called memory. I am so clogged with memories it's a wonder I can make my way from one side of the room to the other without stumbling. It is not what Shakespeare said about sleep knitting up the raveled sleeve of care. I have had a vitrectomy in one of my eyes, that cleared out all the floaters. That eye is invisible to itself, while the other keeps waving itself in front of me saying here I am, see, which is like memory. In sleep, the memories get to run around loose on their own. I think they get tired of being understood.

On Kissing

I don't know why people think it's sexy to suck-kiss as if you want to hang on like a lamprey. Think of the lamprey, a sloppy grope that turns out to be a bad dream, a slimy underside, the wide-mouthed kiss of death. The lamprey wants you, it wants you with a vengeance. There is some attraction in that, I admit. A man on YouTube deliberately attached one to his neck and tried to pull it off. It slithered through his fingers, still holding on. When he finally broke the suction, the spot was growing bloody. You wake up with that feeling of something wrong. That back when your eyes were still stuck together in the womb, you were all lamprey-like, with your larval-like nerve cord, your gill slits. And here you are. You are still that greedy and that vulnerable. If you press the lamprey-mouth against glass, it looks like a grotesque rose window, its center a rasp that scrapes away flesh. It could have destroyed the Great Lakes, it could have sucked the blood from the trout, from all the bony fish. You have that in you. Yet when you hear that Notre Dame's rose window still stands after the fire, tears come to your eyes. You are turned inside out, the sea inside you so full of joy it sloshes over the

rim. Anyone would want to kiss you in your joyful sorrow. Your lips
would touch softly as butterflies.

On House Cleaning

Today, Tina throws the oriental rugs in a pile, releasing them like
weighty butterflies. Dust flies, her hands raven, sweep the land.
She wears a bandana on her head, she plants her feet wide. She
drinks from her Big Gulp. I put things in their place, she shifts
them according to mysterious urgings. I want a canopy over me,
light filtering in waves, clouds of cat fur upon the floor like breaths.
I want dust to take to the air in minute gestures. On the exposed
heating duct above my head when I am in bed is a small dried
worm. It has been there as long as I remember. Even in death, it has
clung to its home, precarious as it is. The two of us have conspired
to keep the secret of its existence from Tina. In a single stroke, the
world as we know it could be obliterated. This is not my house. I
have hired the guerrillas to conduct their warfare before I knew the
whole cost. I have watched the native trees chopped down, grasses
burned, village huts riddled with bullet holes. The guerrillas no
longer expect my guidance. They are like artificial intelligence:
they have learned to speak among themselves, they give instructions
I have no part in. The small worm and I have become great friends.
We have spoken across the barrier called death, we have seen
governments come and go, waving their banners, parading their
silly guns.

On Fog

I am inside a cloud this morning, all these water crystals turning
the trees to pale shadows. There are five kinds of fog, for the five
ways warm and cold try to sort out their differences without warfare.
Sometimes fog turns to frost, other times it hovers over a valley
in the most beautiful layer. You might think of the beginning of
Mozart's requiem. You might not notice, but there is so much

going on there, the suspension made of pushing and simultaneous resistance. Even a kiss is simultaneous resistance. Even breathing. Just to support the bureau in front of me requires the opposite forces of gravity and the wood of an old tree, its molecules still standing tree-like. Fog can be mental. Ever since my father's death, I am in a fog. There are all these floaters of memory in my eyes, like tiny droplets of water that cause a slight obscuring of the landscape. A bit like in a dream, where nothing is quite fastened down. We think we are fastened, but that idea has always been precarious. Like the butterfly, we have been in a conversation all along with the forces of the universe. There are times of atmospheric convection, when the air is perfectly still. So we don't reckon on the housecleaning, even if we say we do. The height of the inversion boundary may vary, but it is always there, ready to turn over, warm air over cool, causing all sorts of fierce thunderstorms.

On Creeks

When I get to a bridge I stand listening to the burble. Who thought up that word? More of a tinkle, maybe. It's impossible for human vocal cords to get the right sound. Which is comforting in that way, something unattainable, hence magical. Language at the end of its rope frays out to babble, or burble, or tears. Language is a rope meandering over the rocks, around curves, downhill. Going uphill is unnatural, unless you are using what is called uptalk? or "recurrent intonational rises"? There is always a period, real or implied, but sometimes you don't want to get to it. Sometimes you want things to go on meandering. Kid's Creek, between where my father used to live and here, has been "improved." It has been made to meander more, its sides have been widened to allow overflow to sink into the ground, and plants have been added along the sides, all to prevent erosion. He liked me to pause his wheelchair on the little bridges, to watch the water. I watch the water, as an exercise in attention. My dreaminess is partly fake. Really, I do not want to stop for anything. As long as I keep moving. Yet also it is hard to turn away from moving water. It may be because of the rocks on the bottom, the way they remain reflective as they are gradually kissed to a smoothness. Creek-time is thus multilayered so as to become meaningless. We are always looking to make time meaningless so we will relax. Yet the sentences—subject, verb, object—seem to have been scientifically designed to clean out everything but meaning.

On Kayaks

The Oru kayak is made like origami, in that it can fold its wings to a suitcase-size. It is translucent, it can be assembled in ten minutes or less! It is barely there, kissing the water. You float in the middle of nothing, at night, under the vast, under starlight and dust, you are upside down, you are always inverted, your floating held to the earth while your head dreams into the dark energy. Dark energy can be thought of as the "quintessence," or a fifth fundamental force, along with gravity, electromagnetism, and strong and weak nuclear forces. Supposedly. No one knows. You are absolutely stunned by this life in which no one knows much. It is all assemblage and floating. The universe slowed before it picked up speed again. It was stopping to check its equipment. It was going to be music. It had started out with a bang, but then thought of more subtle moves, a heart beating through the aorta, slowing as it enters the ventricles. It was too late for singularity. It had to figure how to go on like this, making butterflies, making fathers, watching the collapse of same, the bass note sadness of humans, their mezzo-soprano wail when their villages are cleaned out by guerrillas. What to do with the humans, who want to drag their fingertips through the water so touchingly, who want to hold something back, even while moving on?

On Inversion

Trout lilies coming up in colonies all over the woods, their softly spotted green. They feed their lines out underground. They bloom their one nodding yellow. The colonies can live for hundreds of years, if anything can anymore. Next come trillium, surging like whitecaps where the sun reaches under the trees. They can live for twenty-five years, their seeds scattered by ants and mice. They are also called toadshade and wake-robin. And birthroot, for their medicinal use during childbirth. The sky and planets could be a dream. Here there are real toads and robins trying again, kissing in their way. The ground is sending up its flags. It says look at me. No, it says don't look, this isn't for you and your clever names. It has turned itself upside down, vulnerable again. You are too fast for it. You don't understand. You and your imaginary gardens, your butterfly emojis. You think you have to do something. You have invented yourself as a person who cleans things up, all the while you are being turned over like loam. Look, if you stop to look, you will start to grieve. If you keep on going, all this will seem like a movie, with breathtaking fadeouts of pistil and stamen. It will all seem sexy without the danger, without the angst. It will be merely beautiful. But now it is purposeful enough to make you cry.

On Crying

When I head for the heart of what I mean, I run into absence, which is softer than a wall, deceptive in that I think it is going to let me in, that I will at last find words, that I will own the space I can't touch. Nevermore can I touch it, I want to say dramatically, like in "The Raven," but I have to confess, my father never was there. I have known shards, glints, paragraphs, whole afternoons. Since I've been an adult, I have not cried in his presence, braced against his absence to me, and now he is everywhere. Species are dying out. If you want to get specific, the Roti Island snake-necked turtle is almost gone. The rhino. The zoo is like language, a place to keep for now what otherwise would disappear. *Disappear* rhymes with *fear, tear,* and *dear.* Oh father mine, I was closer than I seemed. Now I am on the other side of the bars, and if you think animals don't cry, you should read about the rhesus monkey, dogs, even rat pups, when separated from their caretakers. It is not all as scientific as you thought. It is not even all tears. It is a weight like the earth on my chest. *Shh*—I have unfolded the kayak, taken it out in the fog. *Shh*—It is the center of the universe out here. What pours in is forever pouring out.

III

Old Woman in Swimsuit

> Imagine if
> afterwards everything can be pure sensation:
> sugar-fed and alive in its dismantling.
>
> —Lotte L. S.

Old Woman in Swimsuit

I

Who could be in love with her own body
when the mind has grown past it
and hovers always
like a large pike in the watery depths?
Or, a bit of both, mind and pike.
From your Bible, you might recite,
by his knowledge the watery depths
were broken open.
You are finicky that way with language.
Such an old word, *finicky.*
One day here, the next gone.
You are swishing endless detail
like dorsal fins. You conclude,
you polish off, yet beyond the end
of the dock, like heaven, your imagination
still waves its fins. Tone is everything.
You can play the pike in your mind
like a clarinet, or an oboe.
Maybe you can play it
all the forty-nine days it takes for a soul
to leave the body, as the Buddhists say.
Though a fish has three seconds
of memory, and so is eternally present.

2

What does the soul do while it waits?
Does it hover before takeoff,
adjusting its angle, recalling
from its sleep and forgetting

(now a line from Wordsworth!)
the old life, shedding its saggy swimsuit,
sinking like a fish before it rises,
airy with bubbles? Young people think
their bodies have always been attached.
They fly off the end of the dock
in one piece. Old people study
their bodies as if they've never seen them
before. They wade into the shallows.
The crumple of skin along the arm
is how loose one becomes.
Everything, in fact, appears
to be hanging in space, not splendid
or radiant, but singing like the pike.

3

Tall, thin tendrils are working their way
toward the water's surface.
You can look down and see the bed
of grasses they emerge from.
The bottom used to be sand only.
This makes you weigh the value
of proliferation. You do not want
to tangle your legs in the weeds
when you swim. You do not want
that feeling of being subtly
stroked, held back. You want to see
winter kill them all off.
You want to look through the ice,
the withered residue, frozen
in place, or waving lazily underneath,
where the water is unbearable.
You want to see what happens when
there's no one to see what happens.

Brief

The baby birds have been dead awhile, packed
      like muffins in the nest in the porch's upper corner,
            one beak still reaching. You don't want silence.

You don't want this depth, from your stool's height.
      You don't want to be this brief.
            You have these brain cells designed to retrieve

stories. She might have been bringing a worm, but something
      to do with a power line, and she's dead,
            or she comes back, or she's somewhere

in between. Surely there's an available truth,
      something that actually happens inside Schrödinger's box.
            Surely you don't cause the cat to live

or die by looking in. So crass. There is a dreaming going on
      most likely, inside the box, that entangles when you
            look in. Like love coming suddenly

from a blind date. And you know how you can
      begin making that into a whole synchronicity.

The Art of Composition

The man across from me on the plane
is depositing notes one by one on or under the lines, tails pointing up,
or down. His earbuds are letting him know if the moves are right.
From the left margin, he seems to be dragging forth emblems
for certain instruments. No one is hearing
but him. He is a large man, sunglasses shoved to the top of his shaved head
as if he has been recently encouraged out of the dark—
a great whale, drawn by the secret ringing
of the depths.
There is so much I do not know.
There is the word *spiritual*, which seems like a greeting from a distance,
some reverberation where desire and conviction meet.
I am forever watching things make themselves up out of stuff
I can't even hear.
And *beauty*, every time I lean close enough, there is the vertigo.
But now I see he is sending a horizontal line
across what he has made, sweeping measure by measure
over the evidence he has placed on his screen.

Sea Otters

The pup's lying on its mother's stomach, leisurely floating.
The others poke their heads up through the rough.

Button noses. Cute. They're known to groom each other
incessantly: called love in some vocabulary. Yet the male mauls

the female when they mate, bites her nose, draws blood,
holds her under until she almost drowns and sometimes does.

Exciting sex. He takes her food, holds the pups ransom for more.
I don't approve of this violence. The woman holding her child

when the soldier raises his gun doesn't approve of violence,
but it struck. Strikes. The woman isn't concerned with the word

love. Her baby has big eyes and a sweet smell.
There is darling charm in the world, true? And there are slaps,

whispered apologies, clawing and biting. I know that story:
he hit her, he slammed his fist through the door, he kept her

up all night yelling, explaining himself, why he had to hit her.
Because he loves her. The otter grooms her pups night

and day, waiting for the next round, not waiting: but who
doesn't know how pleasure and pain make you feel your own

outline so you can see where you are? It's one then the other,
the one God and the other one surely the same.

A Poem for Objects in My House

How often we see in our small objects their history unfold, ghosts
fogging the edges so that they are never only what they are.
The floor where Wally's dishes used to lie side by side,
beside the two circular patches of wood where there were once
ducts, when this condo was an asylum for the insane. The lost
souls comforted, one might hope, by how things go on, the stylish
furniture, the Christmas cactus in the window. Even the small box
beside my chair was made, I was told, out of a walnut tree
on my grandmother's farm. The farm where my great-grandparents
had slaves, who were freed and given their own property.
That is what I was told. Our lives dissipate and can no longer be
heard, even the cries of the enslaved, the insane. Each night
the stars start over again. On the dresser is a tiny silver pill cup
I keep like a blind person, feeling for what it means. It is stubborn,
refusing to say more. Some cries remain frozen in time by the poets.
Anna Akhmatova stood for seventeen months outside the prison waiting
to get in. Another woman, waiting also, lips blue from the cold,
asked her, "Can you describe this?" "I can," she said. Same stars,
same moon. The news collects itself, squares its shoulders, and speaks.
Eddies and moves on, leaving small objects like divining rods.
We were born into them so we can go down with them to find out
how we want to live. We trace their geometry as if the world
had corners. In the corners are the webs of small spiders almost
lighter than we can see, their planet wavering when the heat comes on.
Nothing lands when it dies, I think. The objects sway a little,
having no idea of flight, no idea of anything passing.

Ode on Sadness

I am not sad for now. It's a lovely evening
         with stars. I can be philosophical, since
I feel more optimistic. One way to alleviate sadness
         is to weave and reweave like Penelope,
in other words, concentrate on the small picture.
         Stuffed bears. When the children fly
to their father's for the summer, you can make
         perfect museums of their rooms, bears
poised on their beds. Yet, sadness remains a big
         floater in the eye. Even on a cruise,
one looks out over the sea and thinks, life is short,
         shouldn't I be happier? How happy
is happy? I invited my secret boyfriend Jay
         to the junior high Sadie Hawkins Day sock hop,
deliriously happy, yet sad that he might have said
         yes out of duty or kindness. That tension
all night, a bow drawn over strings. Also, how
         could Penelope have been entirely sad,
with all those milling suitors? Really? Not one
         caught her eye? For that matter,
the couple in the all-night café in the Hopper painting:
         are they happy or sad? They could be
planning a tryst, or just come from one.
         Tryst is homonym for *trist*, which used to
mean sad. The light in that café is the saddest light
         in the universe—enclosed, too bright,
too much exposed. Yet I am trying to hold sadness
         to the light, because I have felt my heart
get so heavy the air has stopped to wait. Even
         thus, even then, I have to say, there was

a shimmering, like stars, inside the sadness.
　　　A delicacy. A sense that I could almost
touch what no one could understand but me.

Ode on Bees

The summer populations of flying insects
        have fallen by more than 80 percent
in the past quarter century. This fact
        is a fact I can't think of very long.
Bees are good at holding themselves away
        from my consciousness with their
furry selves. They contort and arch into
        their blooms. When I do think of them,
it is a pure, balsamic sadness, dark
        and rich, which unfortunately draws
them closer as if I were a bloom myself.
        To become optimistic about bees,
I believe, requires math. You have to see
        the math of their bodies as part of
the greater math, the order in which they
        visit flowers demonstrative
of how the work of the universe can be
        flawless. How theories of living are
nothing next to living. Once a bee
        has identified the taste, the smell,
the touch, it flies a figure eight and waggles
        at the crossing. The angle of waggle
points the direction. The speed tells how far
        to go. And bees remember protein
content, level of toxins. And even if they
        die, and the dragonflies die, and
the flies, zero is not nothing, after all:
        it is holding open the door.

Dear Frida Kahlo

I see you, what you want: the world inside out, framed, a ceremony
of sealing the door. Like Julian of Norwich in her nine-by-eleven
cell, flint walls, dirt floor covered with aromatic leaves and rushes.
So close to dying while alive, so everlastingly straight-on. Looking
at you looking at me, Frida, is like dying. It is like gathering the
taut men we've loved while our bodies broke, our hearts broke,
gathering them to a mutual stillness. I half wish you would let me
let go, let go of me with your colors, your shadow mustache, your
bleeding soul. I have suffered enough, myself. I am okay here, now.
Let us leave issues of the soul to Julian. Let God take her below her
prayers to the tender core where the trembling gates stand open. Let
her squeeze down into a lozenge of herself someone could take and
feel better, throat and nose opened, a hint of eucalyptus. You and I,
God help us, do not wish to be cured.

The Goldilocks Zone

Hawksbill turtles are swallowing shards of plastic.
Their guts are full of it. Their guts are wound with string.
They are hanging from nets in mid-ocean.
You have to look at them. You have to look at the slow deaths.
If you don't, you're already not human. You're developing an exoskeleton.
Yesterday, as I was doing my civic duty on the phones, getting out
the vote, a man said, "They're coming for our jobs."
I was thinking of sea turtles, who have nothing to say about it,
who only want to live underneath what we know.
Who only want to slide along, eating sponges.
The hawksbill turtle is down to precious few.
If we have to watch the demise of this earth, well then.
Before the earth, there was a cloud of gas. Then the clumping up.
Heavy parts sank to the center and lighter parts rose to the crust.
Comets and asteroids crashed their icy bodies on the crust,
forming oceans. Where water neither freezes nor evaporates
is called the Goldilocks Zone. Goldilocks chose the middle bear's bed,
but in the original story, she was a grouchy old woman
and the bears were bachelor bears. She jumps out the window
and is never seen again. This is the version the poet
Robert Southey wrote. There are many other versions, one
in which the old woman is impaled on the steeple
of St. Paul's Cathedral. We have luckily been in the middle
where the story has ended happily for some time.
The other versions are out there, like string theory.

Wounded Dog

He'd said *longitude*. I heard *wounded dog*.
You might say this arose as from a fold in time:
the seventeenth-century wounded dog theory
of measuring longitude:
a so-called powder of sympathy that healed
at a distance. Although it caused great pain.
Sprinkle it on a dog's bandage every day at noon in London.
The dog, onboard far at sea, would yelp, which means
"the sun is upon the meridian in London."
The captain would compare that time
to the ship's time to calculate longitude.
My hearing was thus miraculous for its accuracy,
perfect for the dog, especially if it was my first dog,
the one run over on Garth Avenue,
who'd crossed a line I wasn't allowed to.
Or the other dog we had in Little Rock, the hound
named Tripoli who peed on the floor
and was sent supposedly to a farm. A ship is strumming
the longitude as it passes, a sad song
for the lost dogs. I loved those dogs.
I love how the meridians gather at both ends,
how they spread in the middle like a Japanese lantern.
I try to think how the lantern could be suspended,
to shed light on the question of dogs, where they went,
and if they still hurt outside my radius of knowledge.

Peaceable Kingdom

> The wolf did with lambkin dwell in peace
> His grim carnivorous nature there did cease
> ....
> When the great PENN his famous treaty made
> With Indian chief beneath the Elm-tree's shade.
>
> —Edward Hicks, written on the margins of his
> painting *Peaceable Kingdom*

Too much quiet makes you start thinking. The vague sadness
that's always there begins to attach itself to things.
The lion turns to gaze directly into your eyes.

You try not to shut down, but the floodlight is on you,
turning on you from the wilderness of your own heart.
It has always been like this: pieties and accusations.

You can't see what else. There is only a tableau of creatures,
stilled as if to give notice of what they potentially contain.
Teeth, claws, horns. As if there were a flood of immigrants

to be held at the border, the eyes of the children wide
with despair, and you holding up your treaty, to show there's no
use thinking anymore, in the face of such inviolable words.

Stalking the Wild

You should have seen us scooching from the car
with our walkers, me from knee surgery, him
from the accumulations: the back, the hips.
By you I don't mean anyone in particular, only
the you that means someone should be witness
to what happens! Witness to the tender return,
the determined positioning, the elevator ride.
Who would have thought, is another way to say it.
No high drama, no wailing wall, only the slow-
burning aches that bear our names and ride
to the third floor, where we head toward the door,
leaning like two pigeons caught in a wind, greeted
by Wally the cat on his back, his expanse of white
belly waiting to be rubbed if we could reach
down far enough. We both wish to inform you
that the situation has become absurd, absurd!
Surely you recall, we wish you to recall, Tarzan
and Jane calling out across the vines. Wild animal
thrills! Johnny Weissmuller, lock of hair across
his brow like an impulsive boy's. Cavalier.
Who doesn't love cavalier, and what lies under it,
the lone, the arch presentation? We'd like to
see you try it, yourself, with your two hands
on the walker's handles! Watching to lift over
the dangerous oriental rug. Witness, now,
as your eyes must adjust to a fainter light, what
you're in for: the unexplored, the ruins,
the behemoth and leviathan. Good God, the cooling
of magma beneath the forest floor, the mad
crack in the earth's mantle, and the small triangle
of the rug's corner caught like a lapping tongue.

IV

Twenty Letters in Spring

> and the angels grew surprised
> with the quantity
> of contortion, misplacement, and mischance:
>
> —A. R. Ammons

Twenty Letters in Spring

Tuesday, May 14

Trees here are softening into spring. Really, it is the cruelest time.
I am so sorry for the elms, the ash. They have no place to escape,
even their roots sprawled in the fracked groundwater. Sorrow
can't be everything, can it? I write this to you, old friend, because
everything needs a witness. Who hears the wind, who feels the wind
through the white pines, pitch changing with its speed? Who hears
the aspen's percussion? Thoreau said wind is "magnetizing and
electrifying" the trees. Alternating current. A person gets home by
tacking back and forth, catching the wind when it ruffles the lake.
Where is home? Home is where the cowbell sounds on the end of
the dock, where someone loved me by calling. Call and response.
Alternating current can travel long distances, yet it is worthless
unless the light bulb answers. Unless its filament resists the flow.
When the earth is empty, when resistance is reduced to the still-
uprisen mountains, I can imagine them answering the wind, *hello,
hello*, grateful even for the company of what will grind them down.

Wednesday, May 15

The day she told us her news, the wildflowers were more than an
antidote. I can't tell you exactly. They were tipping themselves
into me with their cups. Trillium, spring peepers, trout lilies, false
Solomon's seal, Dutchman's-breeches, squirrel corn. I walked
the entire trail trying to remember the name of the one that was
blooming in abundance, its droopy yellow, fringed at the bottom
like a ballet skirt. You know, you know: that one. As if you could
help me piece together what's needed. Names instead of grief.
Once all has been named, at least there will be that. Cancer is
never quite. Just under, just along the periphery. It sends out
runners. Can send. There were the flowers, I tilted up a few blooms.

I looked into their faces. I was like a crazy woman, looking into their faces, wanting nothing but evidence of their existence. I had no self, my mouth was their mouth. We weren't sending messages, we were too far under the surface for that. The trout lily leaf tasted like snow peas. Everything tasted like everything.

Thursday, May 16

I thought they looked like remains of an ancient ritual, trunks lying on the ground, bare of bark, etched in intricate patterns, chewed by ash borer larvae. Woodpeckers do love the larvae, but can't keep up. Because the urge to live is like a giant wave, unstoppable. In the case of the ash borer, it has been loosed from its tether, allowed to cross the ocean. At the same time, one thousand hatchling turtles are setting out, and only one will survive. I could say it is beautiful the way each thing fits into the next, the living and dying, the eating and eaten. There are so many protocols against the cancer, so many tests and chemicals to be tried. I say beautiful because it is morning and I am less crazy. Nothing has swallowed me. Overnight the wave has pulled back to let the tiny turtles swim. They will swim for years, whereabouts unknown, before they return. If they return. If they live that long, then they could live a century. I have studied this. There are holes in the universe that let some things through. I report this to you, friend, as a wish that could come true.

Friday, May 17

I was scratching my tailbone, and I felt how I am fastened together. I was seeing my skeleton in my mind. It is as if I have an alien being inside me, which is somewhat the truth. I remembered seeing a photo of a cow someone had blow-dried, for fun. A big, fluffy cow. I didn't think that was funny at all. Poor cow. But then, she might have liked the warmth, the attention. She might have thought of herself as her insides, mostly. What happened to her out there was just noise, scratching across the surface, like news from Venezuela.

If I didn't write to you, would I exist? What does it mean, to exist? I see you perfectly in my mind, though it has been years. Sea turtles see in some way the place they were born. Not as a body of land. More like how the body feels when it is again aligned with the magnetic field that fits it. As if they were stamped out like puzzle pieces. Everything fits. It is not the Eye of God eyeing everything from a long way off. I think not. More like tendons that maintain exactly the right tension to keep the bones in place.

Saturday, May 18

Maybe I'm not just writing to you. The beam from a lighthouse picks up anything within its arc. It is prisms and lenses that make the light bigger than its source, which I take to mean cogitating (my grandfather's word). There is a gospel song about a lighthouse, that brings me back to the Eye of God image, which is hard to avoid, since it's hard to imagine that there is no point. Conversely, where would the lighthouse be if there were no ships? Not everyone is rescued. I am sending this beam in my dear child's direction, crying There! There are rocks! Go this way. The wind (Did I mention the wind?) is crazy. I just tell her what she already knows. I keep trying to act like a lighthouse, but consider where I'm coming from. I am stupid and half-blind myself. If the light is to be amplified, it will have to figure out how, by itself. Everything radiates. Radiation travels in all directions and can break chemical bonds, for good or ill. There is sunlight, and also wild cells. Suppose you wanted to zap something. Suppose you wanted to smash it to smithereens.

Sunday, May 19

I thought it was spring peepers, yesterday, because of the marshy area, but the trill was from the redwing blackbird that landed on the wire. I saw the red flash. Answer came from the tree, so high I couldn't find it. How exciting it was to walk between signals. I was getting electricity from them. He was fluffing his wings, they had their language. Nothing I could say would matter. My idea of spring is cliché, with birds' names and beginning-again. Even my vowels and consonants. All that work, while the birds just push the sound straight out, through their syrinx. I study things. Everything I say is like a prayer carefully shaped to work its way through the impossible materials. Years later all this will be resolved. By all this, I mean what it was I thought the words would do. I was walking beside the cattails. Have you ever broken one open? It's an explosion. You're lost in a rampant cloud. You can cook and eat them. You can even batter them like a corn dog. Transubstantiation goes on all the time, but it's hard to say if anything is lost or gained by it. Maybe the back-and-forth is working like an engine.

Wednesday, May 22

Surely weather is tired of being a metaphor. It must feel like a child whose mother never looks at her because she is too busy on her phone. Today's weather is crying, and of course I am making up the crying, because of how I am inside. Which is another reach: insides can't cry. Yesterday at the lake I saw there was a dead deer on the shore, half-dissolved into earth. I get to go on into spring, I thought, while over the winter the deer has become a part of the firmament. I tried to stitch together the two worlds as if there were two worlds. What if every particle in this world has a partner in another one? If each is metaphor for the other, are they both real? I am only trying to understand space, meaning heaven. Where do we *go?* I am not settling for dispersal. The sign on the bus stop under my window says Downtown in 15, which I take to mean life is short. I too want to go downtown, where the lights are brighter. I too want the two worlds to join their lumens in the way of votive candles in front of a saint.

Thursday, May 23

I did not have a drunk father, a suicidal mother, a stoned brother who went to jail for grand larceny. Where I grew up were petunias, and people mowing. I say that so you won't think I am trying to be a dramatic character in my life. I couldn't see trouble coming because it was already there. It was always too late to fix. In the third grade I kissed a boy. The teacher scolded me and told my mother. I kissed him because it was raining, there was recess at the back of the room, and he wanted to kiss. It is like a blueprint we're given. I add up the reasons, I pretend they explain, but things can happen, anyway: a few mad cells could start inexplicably rattling the chain-link fence you've trusted all your life. You could be that close to having your heart broken. They could keep on until the siren sounds. Prison break! Today the sun is shining. Maybe it will warm up. Maybe there is an appetite for reform today. If everyone had a job and health care. I planted the yellow tulips given to me by a friend. I used a spoon, I didn't have a trowel. They had quit blooming, but they deserved another chance.

Saturday, May 25

I was watching myself tie my shoes. Who thought that up, the way the little half hitches loop and hold? Graduate students have published a paper on why shoelaces come untied. Sometimes it's the way the original knot was formed, under instead of over, or vice versa. What if you do everything right, and still? There is slippage. The handyman Jesus put back all the heavy rocks that fell into the lake over the winter, for only $150. "Jesus saves!" I thought, and then I thought, "That's not nice of me." What a tangled web. In my defense, even DNA forms knots. It knots, breaks, heals itself. The healing sends out free radicals. Even if you do everything right. You could think *time bomb*, but things change so fast, maybe it's closer to a string of firecrackers lit all at once. This is how I cope, going on about firecrackers. If we were face-to-face, you would see the truth. I am softening my gaze, trying for "spirit eyes." If you asked me what I meant, I would say, "Oh, nothing." Not waiting, just hanging out, smoothing the terrain, so it's less likely to trip up, oh, anyone.

Friday, May 31

I have no player anymore for the 45s in my closet. I have kept them
for the same reason I write to you, old friend: we are rolling the
same old songs around in our mouths, waiting to become ghosts.
Meanwhile, we're useful sometimes at *Jeopardy!* In *Jeopardy!*, the
answers are given. Answers are everywhere: desk, swinging bridge,
birth, death. They arrive in response. My desk came from the past
to answer what holds up books, paper, computer. Came from oak
tree. Oak trees can live for four hundred years, they grow so slowly,
collecting their wounds, their furrowed bark, tossing their acorns!
The elements are always changing into one another. "It is natural,"
said Marcus Aurelius, "so why are humans so afraid of this?" The
universe likes to change from becoming to being for a while, to get
to know itself. It changed into "Garden Party," by Ricky Nelson,
on my 45. What I remember, with no player, no needle, is: "If
memories were all I sang, I'd rather drive a truck." On the other side
is "So Long Mama." Mama is out the door, and I can't remember
if that was good or bad, good and bad have changed sides so many
times.

Sunday, June 2

I was putting my bite splint away and I noticed how soft the rug
is, the steel-gray rug at the bathroom sink. Your feet sink in. How
beloved I am, to be so caressed, so free and well-favored. I could
have been born a pig, crammed in a pen, slaughtered for bacon. As
my soul was floating between beings, how did it know to enter here?
Did it understand what else it was letting itself in for? What kind
of stoic the soul must be, to assent to such grief! If it is climbing a
ladder toward enlightenment, what sort of way station am I? I like
it here, my toes in the rug, sun striped on the wall, my heart so
full of trouble I clench my teeth when I sleep. If I were drifting in
intergalactic space, I would want to land here. Once you learn the
language you can turn the heat up or down, you can add notations.

You can invent cures. You have to hurry with that, because life is short. You have to hurry and not hurry. You don't want to miss any more than you have to. Already the forsythia has turned from its startling yellow to green. The greens have deepened all over, and the mowers are trying to keep things civilized.

Monday, June 3

Cure also means salting, drying, or smoking. Meanings can shift sideways, preserving the essence. Such a beautiful day we had yesterday, pulling out the old cottage furniture again. One rotten board. Even hammering is a caress, holding the nail in position, bam, bam, bam! Everything is fastened to everything else in the universe. The fix is always temporary, against the motion. Yet the hands, the screwdriver to pry open the paint can, the brush, the touch—the longing, the pleasure in the damage, in the peeling! "Let your soul stand cool and composed before a million universes," said Walt, all uncool, all onward-and-outward. Such pleasure in the uncool, you wonder how the planets can stand it, riding chilled in their orbits. Meanwhile, I stay close, here, my heart waiting in its thump-thump way for answers to the human questions, like the cure for cancer. Meanwhile, Walt is "bearing the bandages, water and sponge," to the long rows of cots, the gangrenous wounded, faithful to the beautiful language of it, caught fire in his breast.

Tuesday, June 4

Heart as the collection-and-dispersal machine for blood is why it makes a good metaphor. *My heart burns, my heart hurts, she breaks my heart.* I have noticed when the heart gets pummeled enough times, like the piece of meat it is, it softens. Either that or it builds a shell and listens to the hammering from inside its echo chamber. *Breaking* is a horse that bucks until it's tired, blow after blow, hooves on dirt, rearing up, rearing up, oh no, oh no, not this, not this. At last it is horse-and-rider, off into the sunset, and

grief is finally at peace with itself. The road rushes, branches leap.
You keep dodging. Which one are you? On TV news, the mother
combs the rubble for a small doll, any link. This is how I know we
are built to endure. How *soft* means long after. Her hands reach
into the sightless dread; she squeezes herself into the space between
lashes. Nothing comes up, abandonment more and more complete,
more and more like a bruise. The heart is in the shifting purple to
greenish yellow. Like after a bombing, the courageous blossoms.

Thursday, June 6

Nine years ago, when her young son asked if she was going to die,
she said, "Not today." Only so much can be cut away and still be
called "today." I'm starting this to you today, but will only have time
for a few sentences. When you read it, it will be done. If the clock
hadn't been invented, there would still be the sun, the stars, the
longing for early or late, even while time speeds and bends, made
of the same fabric as space. It's hard to picture the silky folds of
space-time. What she meant was, *this is all*. Or, *don't be afraid*. Or,
it will always be today. The intervening years are gone, but memory
lives in the fold, in the droop of fabric that catches what passes.
What a jumble in there, nothing where it used to be! When I write
to you, I have you in mind, but you are a little bit invented, because
of the droop. I am also imagining what will happen with her, now
that the ends have gathered together. Have brought the surprise of
recurrence. When what could always happen, happens.

Friday, June 7

I was flapping out the clean sheets to remake the bed. White as
souls. But aren't souls fat with DNA, sooty with it? We're born with
trouble in our bones, might be a way of putting it. On the bright
side, we're born. How exciting: emergence from the ether, however
temporary! I wonder how gentle the ether will be, upon reentry?
I don't even know what the ether is made of. One doesn't wonder

until it comes close, almost tangible. When the bed's all made, orange throw pillows arranged, these questions seem hopelessly abstract. When she gets the test results, suddenly bones and tissue will announce themselves again, as real as her face in the mirror. I know this. I have been there, as you know. The border between us is questionable. The border is questionable. It is built of so many materials, already breaking down. It is tender as skin. Half a millimeter between us and disaster. Half a millimeter, of nerve endings, exquisite, longing to be stroked, to be held.

Monday, June 10

Rain again, cobwebs on the outside corner of the window are blowing in the breeze but hanging on. Will we hear today? Is it better to know? Humans are ravenous, looking under every stone. No, that seems to be true, but is not. There is deflecting, avoiding. We have lived so long inside our house of dreams, there is graffiti on the walls. Only death pierces the walls, or sneaks in the window. There are windows. I have seen them. Bright openings: oh, this is it! This living is what is actually happening, without Post-it Notes to explain. Bright openings where everything comes to a head, the crest of a wave. I can't think of how to say this to you. When I wasn't looking, wind blew the cobweb so that only a ragged corner is hanging. The once-silky strands, what the spider wrote, tangled with dust, blown down. I would like to see everything, but sometimes I look away. When I write to you, I see you. Am I looking at, or looking away? I don't want to make things worse, either way.

Monday, June 17

What have humans learned, I wonder? That the sky's blue is a wide scattering of the air's molecules? What have we learned about scattering? That it can also be what travels inside the body. What is scattered? Whatever is fighting to win. What is winning now? The opposite of what is wanted. Nonetheless, the sky is blue, spring

beauties are scattered along the path: blue in both directions. She
writes that the right kind of cell receptors are hoped for. *Blue* needs
the eye, the mind, the air. I could have told her, nothing is itself
without everything else. "We'll Understand It Better By and By"
is the gospel song. As if the mind could pierce the endless net of
causes. Write back soon, my friend. Nothing I can say is enough.
I am like a Rothko painting, intense translucence, *orange*, maybe,
going nowhere until I crash against, say, *blue*, the one he invented.
"Without monsters and gods, art cannot enact a drama," he said. Be
my god, then.

Wednesday, June 19

An announcement of cures, to be based on what will be found next!
Triple-negative receptors = chemo forever; triple-negative with PDL
marker = experimental drug; positive receptors = Ibrance. I imagine
tiny Velcro hooks, nubby side or rough. I cannot say I understand,
but how gloriously the words gather fear into little packets! You could
pick them up, turn them to the light as if they were exotic turtles.
Turtles live long lives. They can live on land or water. The mother
lays hundreds of eggs and leaves them to fend for themselves. The
mind draws the words in, little hatchlings, and teaches them what
they are. I would like to get them marching in a straight line, but
by the time they reach you they have begun to scatter themselves
across the sand, into the mouths of wild dogs, foxes, racoons, vultures,
crows, seagulls, ghost crabs. You can catch a ghost crab by sticking
a stick down their hole. It will grab on. Then what? You have this
translucent little bugger at the end of your stick. Maybe you could
save a turtle, but you'd have to kill the crab.

Saturday, June 22

What about the things that are too numerous to have names? Feral
cats. Leaves. Sand. Namelessness is bigger than us. The effort to
claim that something *is* something, or *does* something requires

a hushed, solitary concentration. Oddly futile, because a name
is either too simple or too loaded to mean a great deal. Wanting
exactness carries with it some irony. If you see that all things are
defined by their opposite—no light without darkness—you realize
God is the ultimate ironist: "Oh yeah, I'll call this light, but you
know what *that* means." Sunlight is bright and clear this morning,
laid on the floor, the walls, in painterly patches. The Phillies finally
won yesterday, she texted. You could say I'm calling this much out
from the darkness. Darkness draws an outline around light, and vice
versa. The contrast is the only way we find our way around in this
unknown sea. Words are like little lasers, tacking down the edges. I
had my detached retina tacked down that way, and happily, I can see.

Sunday, June 23

In *Get Low*, Robert Duvall stands looking into the woods where
his long-dead married lover has appeared in a white gown. By this
we know he's going to die. There is the expectation of reuniting—a
symbol for completion—ends brought to meet ends, like a folded
top sheet. The fitted sheet is another story. It is crinkled, crammed,
bunched. When I write to you, think of what doesn't fit! Outside my
assemblage of words may be exactly what's needed to make sense of
everything. I am trying to understand what is meant by love. What
you feel for a child, for example, is more like Einstein's spooky
action at a distance, as if you're connected by some mysterious
communication channel. So many small particles are like this,
it makes me believe in prayer, not so much words but more like
stepping into the entanglement and starting up good vibrations, the
way those words make me start singing the Beach Boys song in my
head. I'm pretty sure you can't step into the entanglement, though.
You're already a part of it.

V

Damage

I tried to drown my sorrows, but the
bastards learned how to swim, and now I am
overwhelmed by this decent and good feeling.

—Attributed to Frida Kahlo

Damage

The nail has split vertically and won't heal. It snags on my pocket.
Age causes this. The nail must henceforth be repaired by a manicurist.

The word *henceforth* shows my age. The nail is evidence that I'm
hopelessly woven into the eternal fabric. Another is my sprained

rotator cuff. On a broader scale, you could include PTSD, impressive
in its desire to replicate fear and misery. The weaving is called

karma—one action triggers another, but appears from so deep it is like
a hand rising from a bottomless pool, brandishing a sword. The rising

and falling always seem original, no matter how many times. The dolphin
is woven into the sea, then into the sky, blowing one out of the other,

just to maintain. There is a photo of me in pigtails, swinging on the catalpa
tree in the backyard. I remember her. She rose out of somewhere

the way a bottle washes up from a thousand miles offshore and will be
pulled away in the next tide. Dreams are the real thing, I know this

because of the havoc they wreak, because of the word *wreak*, which flings
real objects at other objects until someone's dead. Then we're back

where we started, and yet we keep on. A sermon on this makes no
difference. The mind is a sky with clouds woven from nothing, dissolving

as we watch. Persephone got dragged down what I envision
as a deep crack in the earth, narrower and narrower, but then

opening into a room with a bed that would have remained undisturbed
but for the light up there in memory, gradually making itself visible,

because everything up there was dreaming of being made whole.

Joy

What a mess! In Mary Cassatt's *The Boating Party*,
the woman's holding a baby while the rower's

rowing, even though the sail is filled! And he's
facing the wrong way! And waves are washing

all directions! Nothing's one-sided: for example,
two robins out there are acting exactly like robins,

and chickadees keep scrupulously tapping at
the feeder. Nothing wrong or right: my mother still

alive, and not, the way it is when you can't help it,
which is always. The chipmunk she calls "Chippie"

dashes out, then stows himself under the porch.
Years conflate into a wonder-smashing glory.

Nothing to be done. No matter what, you've got
stones, buds, shrubs, hills, tumbling over each other,

sun on this side, naming the shade, each banking
against the sky, coming in for a landing. And

my mother is still in the rowboat, how she loved
to be rowed! I, at least, the bearer of that comfort,

though such recollections can scarcely be endured,
they are so laced with terror and awe, so each

and neither. Yet she is dragging her hand
in the sparkles, joy, for once, at her command.

Letter from Battle Creek

It was the sickly smell of paint from the Chrysler plant
I remember in that marriage. Now these tsunamis,
tornadoes, floods, soldiers packaged like presents
home. I thought I would die from the paint, and the mist

of poison in my sprayer, the wind pushing it across my face.
That nothing would be saved. I picked a particular cause:
shrubs with bagworms clinging to their cedary disguise,
one of them oozing yellow between my fingers. So much

I could say about that marriage. And the way this spring
is coming on loose, as if it's forgetting the regulations.
Not cruel, but raw, a splintered robin's egg. It's the old
smell that comes to me walking along Battle Creek,

still flowing between its expensively manicured banks
left behind by the Kellogg Company when they moved
to Brazil. Still flowing behind empty streets, haunted
by the ghost of commerce. Further down, grocery bags

and beer cans collect in downed limbs. There's a man
under a tree drinking out of a paper bag. I recall the sweet
chemical smell on my hands, how I was dead wrong, then.
Things survive until they can't recognize themselves.

Love Song Including Moon

The full moon has punched a hole in our window.
We are trying to sleep but it is all over us, pale rider, wild.
Shadows are also collaborating, wallows and seepings.
The room is like a negative of a room.
By three o'clock it is coming in a different window.
We have rotated on this raft while we did sleep.
Dear heart, dear heart, will we stop in the morning?

How will we adjust to the two other moons, recently discovered?
The old collisions, the splinterings, still
hanging with us, circling between heaven and earth.

It is all so dangerous, and the reminder in the morning!
The big moon starving after such plenty.

Who can think about the moon for very long? It's good for poems
and lovers, but what if you've been married for years?
Good for astonishment, but then it goes on,
leaving you barely enough
to go to the bathroom without turning on the light.
I see you, wearing your paleness, your reverse self slowly crossing
the bottom of the bed. You are walking on the moon.
The powder of asteroids and meteors is on you
as if you were a baby, old man, bent on not waking me up.

Flying through a Hole in the Storm

The plane shudders and shakes and lurches.
Outside, lightning, exposed, then buried by clouds.
The lady next to you has a dying sister,
and takeoff was long delayed, and you don't ask
if it might be too late. You are thinking
of the German plane crashed in the Alps by the copilot
who wanted to die and take everyone with him
and you're thinking how living is always lit against
the dark and you think there I go again making
metaphor while the lady sits there while lightning
connects the plus at the top of the cloud
with the minus at the bottom as if the cloud were
at war with itself, driving itself crazy trying to reconcile.
You have a sense of flying through space
which is funny because you always are, as surely
as if you were Saint Francis flapping your habit
down the road, keeping nothing, giving away even
what you need, smiling at the lack, the beautiful
emptiness that allows birds to fly through, even
through clouds, and allows for the forest
to be clothed for its creatures and you one
of its creatures, with the kind of raw attention
that can turn to the lady, shedding everything else.
Saint Francis and his monks are heading down
the road, joyful and homeless. You feel the attraction
of homelessness to those with homes, the wish
to be free, to be weightless, but always as
an in-between state, with a fire someplace, a hearth,
a sister. Still, the mind doesn't shake it off,
the plane not arriving, heaven not coming on earth,
and what it must look like from out there at night,
this lone vessel carrying on with its small lights.

Floater

The three-year-old Syrian boy is a floater
               in my eye, sliding
           in front of my vision, limp

body on the sand. His family wanted to get
               to Greece, anywhere
           away from the guns. But guns are bigger

than the ocean. They are driving out
               the Hordes. They are blasting
           at tiny rubber boats, smashing

the face off a mother, leaving
               grandparents in their own
           blood. They turn my chin so I have

to look, while the boy on the sand
               slides on the edge, his small
           shoes, the dusky tint of his closed

lids, the slight movement of his body
               by waves, more terrible than
           stillness. He is one rough disorder on such

a small scale it might be missed. Of course
               there are others: at least
           forty-eight human genetic disorders, tiny,

hidden, working their damage through
               the system, maiming, killing
           in peculiar ways. Still, it's possible to feel

some sense of encouragement in what
                    survives, even in the wince
            of sorrow (the body on the edge of

the sea): how skillfully the eyes take it in
                    and make it a new home.

Dear Grandma Moses

Re: *The Quilting Bee*

I want you to know I am trying, for God's sake, to get back inside
the life we belong in, the old-timey life, the quilting-bee one, with
stitching, sitting, playing with the dog, pouring tea, everyone busy,
no one shooting anyone, no one maimed or dying of starvation, no
one raping anyone, no screeching tires getting away, no one with a
tattooed swastika. I am trying to quit chewing my cuticles. Thank
you for not leaving time in your painting for cuticles, thank you for
putting my hands to good work with the slow stitches, and carrying
the bucket and churning ice cream. Thank you also for not having
learned the art of perspective, since what good is heaven if you can't
see the hand in front of your face? Shapes, colors, only what's given:
a quilt square cut from a dress, a curtain, a flour sack, flattened,
sewn into the whole, to be thrown over someone's bed to keep out
the cold. It is all the small instances that have taken the steady
piercing until the soul is downright visible.

Atmospheric Optics

Bits of clamshell have steeped in the lake for years.
They are small as baby teeth in my palm, and still iridescent.
You would think not,
but the calcium layer is close to the wavelength of light.
Layer after layer causes interference effects,
making its lasting rainbow.
This is about light, but it's easy to forget that.
It's called atmospheric optics.
Everything needs cooperation to make it seem real.
Where did my children's baby teeth go?
Where did my father's leg go
after they cut it off?
You can't help wondering about the tangible quality
of these things, even when they're not pleasant.
The children's wounds, they are so lovely
with their wounds, not visible to the naked eye.
The eye is heavily clothed.
Clams used to live abundantly in the lake.
I have heard stories of clambakes on the wide beach,
which is now gone because of the dam.
Judge Miller and his guitar and the campfire songs.
Ubi sunt? Latin disappeared, too. There are people trying
to bring it back, a boutique effort, at best.
But look at how it turned into Italian, Portuguese, Spanish,
French, and Romanian. It grew lighter and lighter,
breaking into tiny word roots.
All that regret, that sorrow,
fastened in tiny increments to everything,
bending the light. Or, it could be the tears that do that.

Confession

—with a line from the Book of Common Prayer, Rite 1

I used to dream sometimes of a buried body.
I was guilty of something. Afraid of being found out.
I am embarrassed to tell you this. So much is unavailable to me still.
In my dream the earth was disturbed, behind the house.
It was a feeling, with shovels.
This very day I have flushed a stink bug down the toilet.
Plucked it from its happy home on the Christmas cactus leaf.
Watched its flat little body flail and swirl into the dark.
I acknowledge and bewail my manifold sins.
I saw the people on their knees and thought, those words
might be beautiful enough.
"She is not working up to her potential," Miss Jenkins' note said.
I was thrilled that I had potential. My potential hovered
like crow's wings overhead, with their accompanying
shadow. I am thinking how to word my confession.
I have not yet spoken out of my true mouth.
I have not yet grown spare enough
to fit inside the manifold sins, to be the one who pulls the trigger.
It is true I remained silent as the stink bug rotated in the bowl.
I acknowledge there were no mitigating circumstances.
Desperately I have looked for what to say
to give dignity to the stink bug, and to my living on.
Miss Jenkins said, "Quit talking." She named me.
I was the culprit who held the class five minutes over.
I, who wanted to be loved so much I could not quit talking.

Enjoy

In a nest of curled, dried grass,
a rusted sign, vines climbing its back,
"Torch Café," over "Enjoy Teem,"
a picture of the bottle half-visible above the grass.
The Teem Company supports
the advertisement of Torch Café.
Of course nothing's supporting
anything, because the picture
in my head is restless, shifting,
always on its way already, not
to the Torch Café, which is rust.
But this picture has stopped
here at the side of the road,
to say "Enjoy" and something
else below that, obscured
by grass. It could be "Lemon,"
yes, I think so, the added acid
that "enjoy" seems to crave.
The lips that purse just as
paradise comes into view,
and won't quite let it through.

Resting in the Arms

You can buy fully equipped bunkers! For the apocalypse! Old missile silos two hundred feet underground in the middle of the country, high ceilings, swimming pools, saunas, food for years to come. You can die more slowly than the rest, behind sixteen-ton doors. You can drive there early and get comfortably settled before everyone starts dying. I had a very safe feeling in Alaska, in Glacier Bay, that the pale blue sweep of history would go on, continents would rise and fall, and the tiny scratches on the earth would be absorbed. You could say in the arms of God, but God, too, was melting into, say, my uncle Dick, the hydrogeologist who worried and worried over the fate of the earth until now he is too old and just loves the stupid world. Like this autumn, you could say, the red and yellow leaves giving up, with all their flaming hearts. "Everything must burn," wrote Thomas Merton, as he walked around his silent monastery in the dark, on fire watch. "Everything must burn, my monks," the Buddha said in his Fire Sermon. You might think I mean giving up on us, but I'm pretty sure nothing will happen the way we think.

Running with Knives

Mother said walk with the blade down.
If I fell, it would go through my foot.
Better than in the heart. I could choose
how to injure myself, or die.
My sister takes a drug
that keeps her alive but wrecks
her kidneys. What sort of knife?
Butcher? Stiletto? Serrated bread knife?
Circumstances are all. If I had a sickle,
it might curve back in my face
or more likely take the arm.
Serrations might slow the entry
but would rip the surrounding tissue.
Thank you to mother, for her care,
yet, just the other day I turned
the knife up, blade facing me,
and fast-walked. I was taking it on,
I was carving the air, I was looking
in the face the obliteration
of civilized life. Then I turned the blade
out. I could hit a wall, a tree, think of
the context I don't mention, think
of the reasons! Think of a movie
in which after a brave fight, the hero
at last runs the blade through the enemy.
Sigh of relief. Body carried away.
The camera pans with no sound,
only the low hum of the universe,
also a faint high-pitched scree
that could be tinnitus, or someone far
down the hall left the tea kettle singing

and walked away forever, to get
the sugar. Someone meant to make tea,
someone meant well, there's that.

History Is Not a Great Tree

History is not a great tree. It's more
like a bush, I think, or maybe
a sponge, soaking up and periodically
wringing out. Wow, a tree would mean
you could get to the top, to the upper
branches that would weave
from your weight! It would be broad
from there, and still. You could see
dis-ease roll across like wind over wheat.
The way you see a tenement
from the wide glass of your penthouse.
You could imagine yourself down there,
sleeping in your unwashed clothes,
breathing the factory fumes,
eating what's available at 7-Eleven.
You could almost imagine
dying just from living. Growing fatter
in the process. No wonder the germs
love people, no wonder the germs
are joining hands as if they were
playing red rover. History would be
branching and tangling and translating
down there. It would be growing
improbable and efficient. It might come
by air. It could show up either as
the time-that-was, or as the beginning:
an annunciation, a trumpet you didn't
know you heard, until you did.

Weeping Alaskan Cedar

The weeping Alaskan cedar
looks like a starving
child, its few
shaggy clothes hanging.
It is my favorite right now,
a sister in the weeping
world. They will ask,
what was it like, then,
and I'll say that.
I'll say it had a faint
odor, in passing,
and no one else had stopped.
     I'll say
there was so much evil
the word *evil* was hard to say,
but that the cedar said it.
An emptying,
which amounted to
the same thing. It said
it would wait, and that it would
cast a small shadow
in the meantime.
It said it would be quiet
as long as it takes.

Acknowledgments

"Twenty Letters in Spring," *The American Journal of Poetry*

"Ode on Bees," *Michigan Quarterly Review*

"Wounded Dog," *Alaska Quarterly Review*

"Dear Frida Kahlo," *Aperçus*

"Ode on Terror," "Glasses," *Connotation Press*

"Come Moths," *New Letters*

"Afternoons at the Lake," *The Southern Review; Best American Poetry* (2019)

"Brief," *The Southern Review*

"Damage," "Letter from Battle Creek," *The Gettysburg Review*

"Not Dying," *Numéro Cinq*

"The Art of Composition," "Sing," "Old Woman in Swimsuit," "Museum," *Blackbird*

"Wakened by Crows," *Triquarterly*

"Treatises," *Plume*

"Love Song Including Moon," *South Florida Poetry Journal*

"Stalking the Wild," "Flying through a Hole in the Storm," *Hypertext*

"History Is Not a Great Tree," *Los Angeles Review of Books*

Notes

"Twenty Letters in Spring"

> Thursday, June 6: The description of time is from Delia Owens's *Where the Crawdads Sing* (Random House, 2018).

> Saturday, June 22: The part about the effort to claim something is something, and floating on an unknown sea, is from Colm Tóibín's *On Elizabeth Bishop* (Princeton University Press, 2015). The unknown sea part is from a letter from her to Robert Lowell.

> My deep thanks to my dear friend Sydney Lea, recipient, first reader, and chief encourager of these "letters" during a dark time.

Epigraph for part I is from Yusef Komunyakaa's "Blind Fish" (*The Paris Review*, 2012).

Epigraph for part II is from Emily Dickinson's "After great pain, a formal feeling comes."

Epigraph for part III is from Lotte L. S., "As If to Misread Song" (PoetryNow, 2019).

Epigraph for part IV is from A. R. Ammons's poem "Delight," which first appeared in *Harper's Magazine* in 1973.

Epigraph for part V is commonly attributed to Frida Kahlo.